THE BOOK OF FANTASTIC
ANIMALS

Illustrated by
STEPHEN ADAMS

Written by
JANE CARRUTH

TOM

T

octopus

CONTENTS

INTRODUCTION

One chapter in the exciting story of the animal kingdom began over 270 million years ago when a group of animals emerged from the waters to spend some of their time on land. They were the amphibians, the ancestors of the frogs, toads and newts of today.

Although amphibians lived partially on land, reptiles were the first animals to live a truly land life. They were vertebrates, animals with backbones, and were able to move freely on land and to lay their eggs in sheltered places away from the water. The reptiles adapted well to their surroundings and flourished so successfully that they became the rulers of the world. The Age of Reptiles lasted a long time, but ended when the face of the earth began to change and the great reptiles slowly died out through lack of nourishment.

After the Age of Reptiles came the Age of Mammals. The mammals were vertebrates too, but they were different from the egg-laying reptiles. The females of the species suckled their babies on their milk as soon as the babies were born. They were also warm-blooded and had hair. All the mammals known today have descended from these prehistoric mammals that lived millions of years ago. Not all species of the prehistoric mammals have survived, of course. Some kinds could not adapt themselves quickly enough to the changing conditions over a period of time and so they became extinct. However, many mammal descendants of prehistoric times have survived.

Men who study the fossilized remains of animals of prehistoric times are known as palaentologists and they have been able to tell what the ancestors of many present-day animals looked like. The Bison, for example, was once hunted by men of the Ice Age. These men killed Bison with bows and arrows and, after a day's hunt, they would paint pictures of their prey on the walls of their caves. Another huge animal, the Rhinoceros, is now almost hairless; but its ancestor was covered with thick woolly hair and, like the Bison, was hunted by early man.

Like the Bison and Rhinoceros, all the animals shown in this book have some unusual fact or intriguing characteristic that is fascinating and easily remembered. From the amphibious Treefrog to the famed Indian Cobra to the Three-toed Sloth, fantastic animals are described page by page.

Some words that may be unfamiliar are explained in the glossary at the back of this book.

TREEFROG (male)

Habitat: Africa. **Size:** approx. 1 in.
He has a large vocal pouch.

All frogs are amphibians. They spawn in the water and their larvae are fishlike tadpoles that eventually lose their tails and grow land legs. Although the Treefrog spends all its time in trees, its life begins in the water. These frogs have specially developed feet which enable them to cling, fly-like, to vertical surfaces. Another remarkable thing about the little Treefrog is the way it can change its colour to blend in with its surroundings. The picture shows a male Treefrog inflating his vocal pouch to the size of a balloon as he gives out his harsh, croaking call during the mating season.

FRILLED LIZARD

Habitat: Australasia. **Size:** 3 ft. long, frill 8 in. across.
It has a frilly collar.

Lizards abound in Australasia and the Frilled Lizard is one of the most interesting. As you can see from the picture, it has a pleated membrane covered with spots which it expands like a mediaeval ruff when angry or frightened. At the same time, it opens its big mouth very wide.

These lizards live in trees and feed on insects. When they move about on land, they leave tracks that are said to resemble, in some ways, the tracks left by dinosaurs in prehistoric times.

MOLOCH

Habitat: Australia. **Size:** 8 in. long.
It looks like a miniature monster.

Another lizard of Australia is the Moloch that is found in the deserts and is covered all over with long prickly spines. Looking for all the world like a monster in miniature, the Moloch, or Thorny Devil as it is sometimes called, is nevertheless small enough to sit in the palm of one's hand, and is quite harmless. Despite its small size, however, the Moloch has an insatiable appetite for ants which it catches with its tongue.

There are nearly 3,000 different species of lizard scattered throughout the world, but none more fantastic than the aptly named Thorny Devil.

AFRICAN
HORNED CHAMELEON

Habitat: Africa and Madagascar.
Size: approx. 1 ft. long.
It can change its colour.

Chameleons are known for the fantastic
way in which they can change their
colouring to match their surroundings.
We have borrowed this name and applied
it to people who change their opinions in
a flash to suit their company!
Another fascinating fact about this small
lizard is its remarkable club-shaped tongue
which it shoots out to catch its prey.
When a succulent fly comes within reach, the Chameleon
launches out its long tongue and traps it on the sticky,
club-shaped end. You would never guess that inside the
lizard's mouth lies this long, coiled-up tongue just
waiting to be released.
Like snakes, chameleons lay eggs, sometimes as many as
36 at one time, in a hole in the ground which
is covered over with earth.

INDIAN COBRA

Habitat: India.
Size: approx. 6 ft. long.
It is one of the deadliest snakes.

There are hundreds of different species
of snakes scattered throughout the world.
Among some of the most deadly are the
cobras, including the King and Indian
Cobras that are found in India. The Indian
Cobra is most dangerous at night and when
disturbed, it raises itself into the air and
spreads out its enormous hood to display two
menacing black eye markings. When it does
attack man, the bite is frequently fatal. You
may be surprised to find snake charmers using
Indian Cobras in their acts, but it seems probable
that being a night-time attacker the Indian Cobra
has difficulty in aiming its poison during the day.
Nevertheless, some snake charmers are said to sew
up the mouths of their 'pets', whilst others
may remove the fangs or induce them to
eject the fatal poison into cloth just before
the performance is due to begin.

VAMPIRE BAT

Habitat: Jungles of America.
Size: $2\frac{3}{4}$ in. long.
It is a blood-sucking flying mammal.

Bats are found all over the world and
some kinds can fly almost as well as
birds. The fearsome looking Vampire
Bat of the American jungles is a blood-
sucking bat, but there are fruit-eating
bats and bats that eat insects. Nearly all
bats sleep in the day-time, hanging
head downwards by their claws in dark
caves. Bats have big appetites which they
satisfy during the night hours. Their
fantastic sense of hearing enables them
to avoid collisions in the dark.
And when they fly around they give out bleeps that literally bounce back
at them from any obstacles in their flight path. But these bleeps are too
high-pitched for the human ear to pick up.
One of the strange things about these flying mammals is the way all the
females in one cave give birth to their young almost at the same moment.
Usually only one baby is born and it is blind and naked. The baby clings
to its mother, taking her milk, and growing daily stronger as she carries it
around with her. But not until it is much older does it receive its first
lesson in the art of flying.

MOOSE

Habitat: Yukon, Alaska and Canada. **Size:** male—about 6 ft. high at the shoulder and 1,100–1,200 lbs.; span of antlers: up to 6½ ft.
It is the largest of the deer family.

Biggest and most powerful member of the deer family, the Alaskan Moose, with its fine spread of antlers and breadth of shoulder, is an impressive sight. Found in Eastern Yukon, Alaska and Canada, this giant among deer frequents lakes and rivers and is protected by law.

Moose are fine swimmers and feed on the stems and leaves of water-lillies whilst in the water. They will frequently submerge for quite long spells and then suddenly reappear— to the astonishment of some chance visitor to the lakeside who had no inkling that a herd of Moose were in the water! During the mating season, when his antlers are fully grown, the bull becomes belligerent and aggressive, challenging other males to a fight that sometimes ends in death.

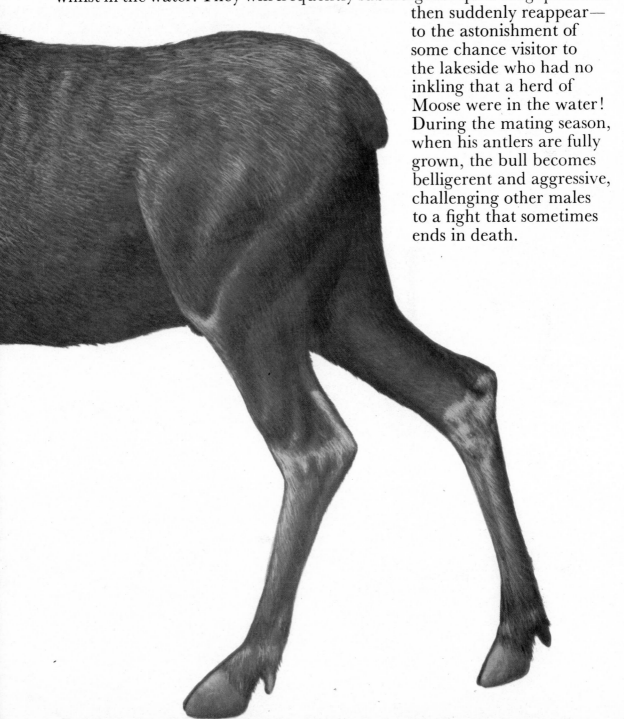

BOTTLE-NOSED DOLPHIN

Habitat: North Atlantic and Mediterranean.
Size: 10–12 ft. long.
It is the most intelligent sea mammal.

Dolphins are cetacean mammals. The word Cetacea is applied to certain mammals that live in the water, including whales and porpoises. It is not always easy to distinguish between a porpoise and a dolphin but, if you are ever in doubt, this picture of the Bottle-nosed Dolphin will serve to remind you that all dolphins' heads end in a beak whereas porpoises are blunt-nosed.

The Bottle-nosed Dolphin, found in the North Atlantic and Mediterranean, is considered to be the most highly intelligent non-human creature and is famous for its ability to respond to training. Affectionate and playful, dolphins swim about the sea in schools, feeding chiefly on fish.

ELEPHANT SEAL

Habitat: South Atlantic Ocean.
Size: male up to 20 ft. long;
females about ½ that size.
It has a snout like an elephant's trunk.

Seals, with walruses and sea lions, form a
group of hairy-skinned animals called
pinnipeds because, in the process of
evolution, their legs and feet have changed
into flippers. They are mammals that have
taken to the sea where they spend most of
their lives, existing on fish.

They return to land, however, to breed.
The Elephant Seal is the biggest of all
seals and its long pendulous snout
looks somewhat like an elephant's
trunk! At one time, Elephant Seals,
or Sea Elephants as they are often
called, were found in vast numbers
on islands in the South Atlantic.
But, as with other species of
seal, their traditional breeding
places became so well known that
it was easy for hunters to search
them out and they were slaughtered
almost to extinction. Today
these magnificent seals are
protected by law.

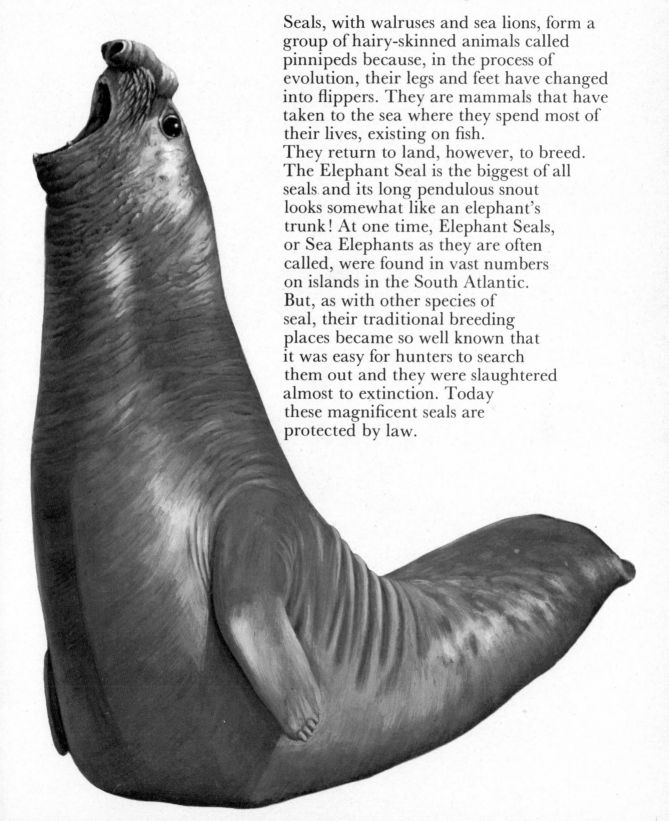

DUCK-BILLED PLATYPUS

Habitat: Australia. **Size:** approx. 20 in. long.
It is one of the few living mammals that lays eggs.

Did you know that the most primitive of all
the mammals are the ones that lay eggs?
One such living mammal is the odd little
Duck-billed Platypus found nowhere
in the world except Australia.
It makes its home in a long burrow
close to a river-bank and here
the female lays her two soft
rubbery eggs.
With its webbed feet, flat
tail and beaked nose, the
Duck-billed Platypus is one
of the strangest looking
creatures in the animal kingdom.
An expert swimmer as well as an
excellent excavator, it dives
for its supper, feeding on
worms and different kinds
of shellfish. Though small
and round, the male has a
nasty temper, especially
during the mating season,
when he uses the poisonous
spurs on his feet to
fight off any rivals.
The Duck-billed Platypus
is among the very rare
mammals of the world.

STAR-NOSED MOLE

Habitat: North America.
Size: 5–6¼ in. long, with tail of equal size.
It has a star-shaped nose!

Built for burrowing, this stubby little creature,
with its curious, star-shaped snout, has a thick
furry coat and round head. Its tiny eyes, buried
in black velvety fur, can just about distinguish
light from dark.
Like all other moles, the Star-nosed Mole lives
underground but close to water where it uses
its long, spade-like fingers to tunnel under
the marshes.
Unlike other moles, the Star-nosed Mole is
a good swimmer when it uses its remarkable
hands like paddles! It has, too, a tail
almost as long as its body, whereas other
species of moles have scarcely any
tail at all!
Generally speaking, moles are unfriendly,
anti-social little animals, but not so
the Star-nosed Mole of North America,
who lives a peaceful, sociable existence
in underground colonies. Active and
always busy, when the Star-nosed Mole
is not swimming, it is tunnelling
energetically in search of the
worms and grubs it so loves to eat.

AARDVARK

Habitat: Africa. **Size:** up to 6 ft. long.
It has very strong claws to break open the termites' nests.

Like the Star-nosed Mole, but found in Africa, the Aardvark has strong digging claws. It is sometimes known as the Ant Bear because of its fondness for ants and termites. Termites' nests are often three times as tall as a man and enormously strong, but they offer no resistance to the Aardvark's powerful claws. As soon as it breaks open the nest, it licks up the insects with its long tongue.

The Aardvark grows to a length of 6 feet and there is something endearingly comic about its appearance, for, although it has the snout that reminds you of a pig, it has ears that make you think of a donkey!

The Boers, when they settled in Africa, called it Aardvark which, in Dutch, means 'earth pig'.

STRIPED SKUNK

Habitat: North America. **Size:** body approx. 1 ft. long.
It has a very effective defence mechanism!

All members of the skunk family go through life with an
unpleasant handicap—their offensive smell which comes
from the glands under their tails. When the skunk is
attacked, it raises its tail so that it can spray
its enemy with evil-smelling liquid which is its
best method of defence. As if to compensate for
its objectionable odour, the Striped Skunk is
extremely attractive in appearance. Its coat is
black and shiny with a white stripe along each
side. If it is roused to anger, it hisses and stamps
its feet as it ejects its fluid.
A native of North America, the Striped Skunk
is rarely seen in the daytime, spending
much of its time underground.
Not surprisingly, it is a
distant cousin of
the weasel.

THREE-BANDED ARMADILLO

Habitat: Brazil and Bolivia. **Size:** 16 in. long.
It has a suit of armour for self-defence.

While the skunk has its evil-smelling liquid for defence, the armadillo is
well-equipped with armour platings. Although fitted out like a knight in
armour, the armadillo's horny plates are joined by flexible skin. This
means that in times of danger it can roll itself into a ball and draw in its
head as well as its feet.

The amount of protective armour that the armadillo carries makes it
comparatively heavy for its size. But if it is attacked by an animal like a
wild dog or a coyote, against whom it has little defence, it will make for
water and swim away to safety. The Three-banded Armadillo in the
picture is found in Brazil and Bolivia where it feeds chiefly on insects.

BLACK RHINOCEROS

Habitat: Africa. **Size:** 12 ft. long and up to 2 tons; horn up to 2 ft. long.
It is one of the most ferocious and aggressive of large animals.

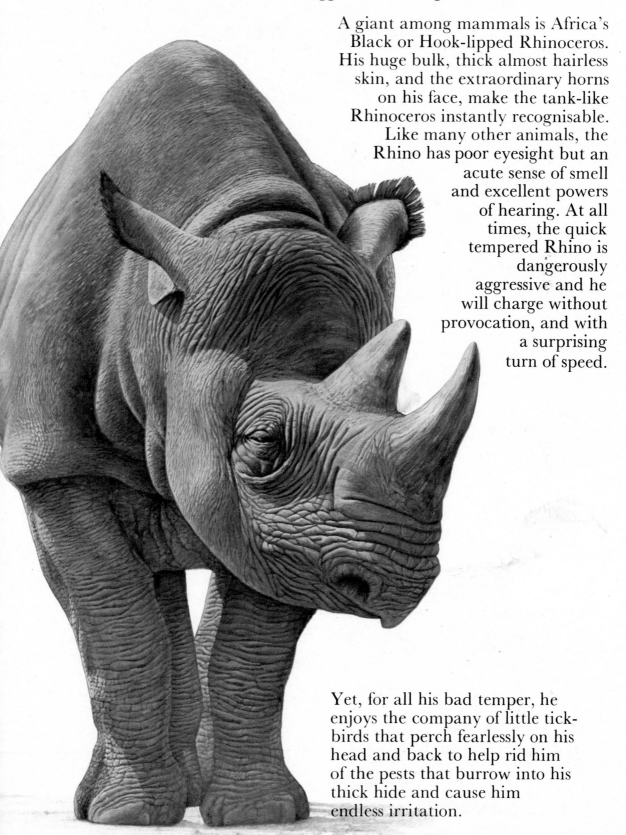

A giant among mammals is Africa's Black or Hook-lipped Rhinoceros. His huge bulk, thick almost hairless skin, and the extraordinary horns on his face, make the tank-like Rhinoceros instantly recognisable. Like many other animals, the Rhino has poor eyesight but an acute sense of smell and excellent powers of hearing. At all times, the quick tempered Rhino is dangerously aggressive and he will charge without provocation, and with a surprising turn of speed.

Yet, for all his bad temper, he enjoys the company of little tick-birds that perch fearlessly on his head and back to help rid him of the pests that burrow into his thick hide and cause him endless irritation.

AMERICAN BISON

Habitat: North America. **Size:** male up to 6 ft. tall and 1½ tons.
They were a source of food, clothing and shelter for the Red Indian tribes.

At any zoo you will almost certainly come across the North American
Bison that once ranged the plains of the Far West in vast herds. Known
in the many stories of the Wild West as Buffalo, they should not be con-
fused with the African Buffalo.

Their most determined enemy was man and to the Indian, Bison herds represented a whole way of life. Rope, tents, clothing and food all came from the shaggy Bison. From time immemorial, the Indians hunted and killed the Bison, but in reasonable numbers until firearms resulted in the wholesale slaughter of the Bison—not only by the Indians, but by the white hunters and settlers.

Today, Bison are kept on Reserves where they are protected by law, and the danger of their extinction has passed.

MUSK OX

Habitat: North America and Greenland. **Size:** up to 5 ft. tall.
It produces a musky smell!

The Musk Ox of North America and Greenland has a coat of long coarse hair that helps it to withstand the bitter cold of the Tundra. The hardiest of animals, they survive the furious Arctic blizzards by huddling together for warmth, and to protect themselves from prowling wolves. Cowlike in appearance, the Musk Ox exists on what roots it can unearth from under the thick snows of the Arctic winter. At one time they were in danger of extinction far more from the Eskimo hunters than from the hungry wolves, but they are now protected in Reserves. Their name, of course, comes from the musky smell that they produce.

GIANT PANDA

Habitat: Western China.
Size: 5 ft. tall.
They are one of the world's rarest yet most loved animals.

In toyshops, Giant Pandas are every-where on the shelves and they rival the teddy bear in popularity. In real life, they are extremely rare and little was known about them until one was taken into captivity in 1937. With its black eyes, black legs and black saddle across its back, the Giant Panda, found only in Western China, is regarded with affectionate interest by children and grown-ups alike. Although it has the build of a brown bear and has thick, bear-like fur, it is more nearly related to the raccoon. In the bamboo jungles of China where Giant Pandas live, they feed mostly on bamboo shoots and small rodents, but in captivity they have been found to eat a more varied diet. Baby Giant Pandas take nearly five years to grow up and are comic and lovable.

BACTRIAN CAMEL

Habitat: Central Asia.
Size: 7 ft. to the top of the humps.
It has two humps which act as a store house for energy.

There are two types of camel, the Bactrian and the
Arabian. The camel in the picture is the Bactrian
Camel and is much heavier and stronger than the
camel found in Arabia, which has only one hump instead
of two. The bigger and more robust Bactrian Camels
are much better suited to the harsher climate and
rocky terrain of Central Asia, their native land. Their
two humps are store-houses of fat and like the Arabian
Camel they can travel long distances without food and
water. Desert travellers will testify to the hardy
endurance of camels, even though they deplore their
bad-temper and mean nature!

The camel's feet are designed for desert travel, with
big soft pads and stout toes. Their long eyelashes
protect their eyes from blowing sand.

GOLDEN LION MARMOSET

Habitat: Tropical jungles
of Brazil.
Size: Head and body 9–14½ in. long,
tail 12–14 in. long.
**It spends much of its time
grooming its long silky hair.**

The Golden Lion Marmoset is one of
the most beautifully coloured of all
living animals. The male is said to
help at the birth of the young and
wash them as they are born. He carries
them for several weeks and pre-chews
all their food for them. Marmosets sleep
for much of the day, but when they are awake
their chief activity is grooming their long manes
with squirrel-like industry! Marmosets are quite often
adopted as pets for they are not hard to tame and have
affectionate natures.

MANDRILL (male)

Habitat: Africa.
Size: male head and body up to 3 ft. long.
He is the largest member of the monkey family.

The Mandrill is the biggest of the monkey family and is found only in Africa. Unlike many of the smaller monkeys, he moves about on all fours. But it is his odd distribution of vivid colours that makes the male Mandrill so memorable. With his bright red and blue face and equally colourful hindquarters, he looks as if he might have stepped out of somebody's nightmare! Although they are quarrelsome and aggressive, Mandrills are at their best inside the family unit. The male will defend his family against an enemy many times his own size, using his strong teeth to great effect. Like all baboons, the name given to large African and Asian monkeys, Mandrills live on the ground, in colonies, feeding on birds' eggs, roots and insects.

PROBOSCIS MONKEY (male)

Habitat: Borneo jungles.
Size: male head and body up to 2 ft. 6 in. long, tail of equal length.
He has a fantastic nose!

For all the world looking like old man Punch himself, the Proboscis Monkey's fantastically long nose is his most unusual feature. As you can see from the picture, it actually overhangs his mouth and measures three inches.
Found in the jungles of Borneo, the Proboscis Monkey is extremely active and travels through the jungle at great speed. These monkeys also have a great liking for water and are good swimmers, swimming paddle-fashion, in much the same way as do dogs.

THREE-TOED SLOTH

Habitat: Central and South America. **Size:** 19½ in. long.
It is the slowest moving mammal.

The sluggish sloth leads a topsy-turvy life, for its favourite and habitual pose is hanging upside down by its hook-like claws from the branch of a tree. If the sloth were to drop to the ground it would be completely helpless, since, with its long curved claws, it has difficulty walking. It is, in fact, the slowest moving mammal on earth, moving over the ground at no more than 0·1 m.p.h. Fortunately, the Three-toed Sloth has a perfect camouflage from its two greatest enemies, the jaguar and the eagle. In the rainy season, as it hangs from a green leafy tree, its coat becomes host to thousands of tiny green plants, known as algae, that grow out of its thick coarse hair. In times of drought, the algae take on a yellowish appearance as do the leaves of the sloth's tree-home.
All through the hot sunny day the sloth, found in Central and South America, hangs motionless. Then, as night falls, it bestirs itself and begins to eat the succulent shoots and leaves that keep it alive.

CHEETAH

Habitat: Persia, Central India and Africa.
Size: up to 8 ft. long including tail.
**It is the world's fastest animal
over short distances.**

From describing the slowest moving mammal on earth, we end our book with one of the fastest. The beautiful, graceful Cheetah or Hunting Leopard is used in the East to hunt deer or antelope, and when running at full stretch its feet scarcely seem to touch the ground. It may reach speeds of between 60–70 m.p.h. over short distances.

Cheetahs are not, as you might imagine, true members of the cat family, for they do not have retractile claws—that is claws that can be completely drawn back. They are found in Persia, Central India and Africa and they are sometimes kept as glamorous and affectionate pets, being easily tamed.

GLOSSARY

amphibian: from the Greek, meaning 'both' and 'life'. Frogs, toads and newts begin life in water, but at a certain stage they leave the water for the land.

cetacean: term that applies to mammals that live in the water and closely resemble fish.

evolution: the gradual process of development of animal life, from the earliest species onwards.

grub: larva of insect

mammal: warm-blooded, air-breathing vertebrate, with fur or hair covering, that suckles its young.

membrane: thin skin.

nocturnal: active in the night.

palaentology: study of extinct fossilized animals.

pinniped: fin-footed animal.

reptile: cold-blooded, egg-laying, scaly-skinned animal.

retractile: capable of withdrawing.

to spawn: to lay eggs in the water, e.g. fish, frog, etc.

venom: poisonous fluid.

vertebrate: animal with a spinal column.

Planned and directed by The Archon Press Limited, 14-18 Ham Yard, London W1
First published 1975 by Octopus Books Limited, 59 Grosvenor Street, London W1

ISBN 0 7064 0337 1

© 1974 The Archon Press Ltd

Distributed in Australia by Rigby Limited
30 North Terrace, Kent Town, Adelaide, South Australia 5067
Printed in Italy
by Stabilimento Grafico Editoriale
Fratelli Spada - Ciampino-Roma